The Last Day

By Robert Hern

Preface

Jesus said, "No one comes to the Father except through me."

(John 14:6)

Is there any hope for those outside salvation by grace through faith in the perfect sacrifice of Jesus Christ?

What kind of salvation did the Jews believe in; were they mistaken?

The realization of "*salvation by grace through faith*" in Jesus as *a free gift* from God was not _publicly_ announced to the masses until the 1500s by Martin Luther. *The Great Awakening* in the 1700s was a milestone, drawing tens of thousands of people to the pulpits by inspiring preachers like Jonathan Edwards, George Whitefield and others.

Think about it. It wasn't *until* 1500 to 1700 years after the Son of God walked on earth till God finally says, "At last, a people after God's own heart. These are the true people of God. Only they will be saved."...... Give me break!

Let's be blunt does God think Christians of today are a better selection, are more worthy, or a more devoted people since the time of Adam and Eve. In fact, prominent Christian leaders are now saying we are entering an age of Christian rebellion. The *Rebellion* is a Biblical prediction in Thessalonians 2:3 describing the beginning of the end.

To be a Christian, one must believe in the death burial and resurrection of Jesus Christ is 100% accurate. Christians are saved by grace through faith in Christ Jesus. Christians will become incorruptible before we can enter heaven to be with God. But, what most preachers don't realize is that they are saying that God has no other plan. These preachers are mistaken.

There are a multitude of mysterious passages from the Bible that cannot be deciphered by theologians; therefore these passages are neglected and at times pushed aside, ignored.

Without realizing it, most Christians are saying that out of 6000 years of Biblical time, beginning when Adam and Eve were thrown out of the Garden of Eden, there has only been a brief period of time to gather a saved people. Salvation by Grace alone was not announced publicly until Martin Luther after the

1500s. This means there has only been about 500 years of productive fruitfulness. During this time a massive number of people were added to the Family of God...... Is this what Christians believe? Come on; now let's take a look at the rest of God's plan. There is much said from the Word of God. The drama is not over, in fact, there is more to come.

This book is written to prove through the Word of God, without nullifying John 14:6, how God will justify many whom He has chosen before the creation predestined for adoption to be holy and blameless, according to His Will and Pleasure. (Ephesians 1)

Table of Contents

An Overview of The Last Day

This *Overview* is not written to intentionally shock the reader but is written to highlight profound Biblical passages. The Word of God is called the Living Word because it has a life of its own. This life within the Words of this book is ordained by God it continues to shed new light at His appointed time. It has taken almost 1600 hundred year after His resurrection for the gospel to be spread throughout the world by massive Bible publication and evangelism. Finally the world realized that through faith by believing in the Son of God, we can be saved and given the right to become children of God.

An Overview of The Last Day

Since the time of Jesus resurrection, men inspired by God, have written the New Testament which completes the entire Bible, the Old and New Testament. The past, present and future for all people of the world is marked within these writings.

By God's designed the scriptures have again opened up to reveal the mystery of the *Last Day* of what we recognize as human existence; to be transformed into something beyond our comprehension. It has taken over twenty years to align mysterious passages which when compiled, revealed an extraordinary glimpse of the future. It has been very difficult in trying to determine which Biblical event to present first and in what order, in an attempt to minimize confusion for the reader.

An Overview of The Last Day

The only possible way to grasp the reader's attention was to present the facts at the very beginning. These facts, scriptures, are tossed at the reader like cold icy water (shock) followed by Bible references and explanation for these conclusions. As you read, it is your responsibility to prove through scripture that these words are scriptural. God always receives all the glory. The Bible is His Word, His message.

An Overview of The Last Day

How do we enter the Kingdom of God? Anyone rejecting salvation through Jesus will lose their opportunity once they die. If flesh and blood cannot inherit the Kingdom of God (1st Cor. 15:50) this means we will exist in a different form with Christ.

Death is final; there is no second chance for those who rejected salvation in Jesus Christ. But what happens to people *worthy of salvation* who never heard the gospel?

According to Leviticus 17:11; the life in God's creation is in the blood.

Jesus shed His blood and died for our sins.

Once creation dies, the blood sheds its life.

Can a person live without blood?

An Overview of The Last Day

You may think this is a ridicules question but what seems impossible for man is not impossible for God.

In Luke 24:39, when Jesus appeared in the presence of the apostles, He had not yet received His glorified body as depicted in Revelation 1:14-16.

He said, "I am not a ghost, handle me for I am flesh and bone."

While they were still talking about this, Jesus himself stood among them and said to them, "Peace be with you."

They were startled and frightened, thinking they saw a ghost. He said to them, "Why are you troubled, and why do doubts rise in your minds? Look at my hands and my feet. It is I myself! Touch me and see; a ghost does not have flesh and bones, as you see I have."

An Overview of The Last Day

When he had said this, he showed them his hands and feet. And while they still did not believe it because of joy and amazement, he asked them, "Do you have anything here to eat?" They gave him a piece of broiled fish, and he took it and ate it in their presence.

The Least in the Kingdom of Heaven

It is interesting to note in this passage, that Jesus tells His disciples that John the Baptist is the Greatest of all Prophets. (I thought Moses was the greatest.) At this point John has been beheaded and Jesus makes a strange compelling statement.

Here is the mystery, Jesus said in Matthew 11:11

"Assuredly, I say to you, among those born of women there has not risen one greater than John the Baptist; _but_ he who is _least_ in the kingdom of heaven _is greater than he_.

The Kingdom of Heaven is where God dwells. Jesus said He is going to prepare a place for Christians in Heaven to be with God.

The Least in the Kingdom of Heaven

Who will go to heaven? It is they who live by faith and build upon the foundation of Jesus Christ

Now if anyone builds on this foundation *with* gold, silver, precious stones, wood, hay, _or_ straw, each one's work will become clear; for the Day will declare it, because it will be revealed by _fire_; and the fire will test each one's work, of what sort it is. If anyone's work which he has built on *it endures*, he will receive a reward. If anyone's work is burned, he will suffer loss; but he himself will be saved, yet so as through fire. (1st Cor.3:12)

Consider the _least_ in the Kingdom of Heaven is the one using straw to build on the foundation of Jesus. Even though his work counts for nothing, they will be saved.

8.

The Least in the Kingdom of Heaven

Jesus said John is already dead; there are none greater than John.

But the least in heaven is greater?

There is something missing, something none of us Christians understand, much less able to explain.

But Jesus said the <u>least</u> in the Kingdom of Heaven is greater than he.

If John the Baptist is lower than "<u>*the least*</u>" in the heaven. The least means the last one; there is no one left. Therefore according to Jesus, John will not be in the Kingdom of Heaven, it is only for Christians. John is not condemned yet he is not in heaven where is he?

The Least in the Kingdom of Heaven

In order to be a Christian one must believe in the death, burial and resurrection of Jesus Christ. John didn't know Jesus would be crucified. John was never aware of perfect sacrifice of Jesus and salvation through the blood of Christ.

What was John the Baptist, like all the other Jews were waiting for? Were they waiting for an Old Testament Promise from God?

This was one of the first of many mysteries I held for over twenty five years.

It began a search in collecting pieces of the puzzle that could only be revealed through the Bible by God.

The Least in the Kingdom of Heaven

If there are none greater than John the Baptize before the resurrection of Christ and the least in Heaven _is_ greater than he, *who are the greater*? They are the Christians.

John the Baptist, just as many descendants of Israel, were waiting for the Messiah and The Kingdom of God, an earthly government. The Christ was to be seated on the throne of David.
(Isaiah 9, Luke 1:32)

They didn't expect *The Christ* to be crucified

The Least in the Kingdom of Heaven

Paul said in Romans 11, has God rejected the Jew? Certainly not!

The question is, how will God preserve the Jews from destruction if they are _lower than the least_ in the Kingdom of Heaven, what will happen to them if they are not allowed in heaven?

HE SAID TO THEM, "THIS IS WHAT I TOLD YOU WHILE I WAS STILL WITH YOU: EVERYTHING MUST BE FULFILLED THAT IS WRITTEN ABOUT ME IN THE LAW OF MOSES, THE PROPHETS AND THE PSALMS." (Luke 24:44)

The Least in the Kingdom of Heaven

Why was Jesus not in His Glorified body, is this a clue? In the presence of God, Adam said of Eve, "this is flesh of my flesh bone of my bone." They lived on earth in the Garden of Eden. Will people be like Christ as He appeared to the apostles in flesh and bone? Are people given life by God's breath? If the Kingdom of God is on earth, who will inherit it?

The Bible mentions those who are not dead but sleep _until_..... In Ezekiel 37, there will come a day when tendons, flesh and skin is returned to dried bones of His people. Will they be flesh and bone? Then God gives them the breath of life.

The Least in the Kingdom of Heaven

Are these the answers to many questions concerning the Millennia, a time when *Satan is bound and Christ rules the world? (Revelation 20, Zechariah 14)* Is it a physical Kingdom? *This takeover of the world will become a Kingdom belonging to God, The Kingdom of God.* There is significant scriptural evidence proving that God has predestined a select people, *to be born again* by His own breath *to be justified* by giving them an opportunity in the Kingdom of God, to know the King of the Jews during the Millennial Reign of Christ. (Zech. :14, Rev. :20)

They, who are given God's breath to live again, are not saved as Christians who are by the blood of the Jesus are free from sin.

The Least in the Kingdom of Heaven

How can one believe unless one has heard the gospel? (John 14:6) In order to be saved, one must confess that he believes that Jesus is the Son of God. Those who are regenerated with God's Breath during the Millennium, both Jew and gentile, never heard the gospel; they still carry their sins, they are the sheep. During the Millennia they are still ignorant of the resurrection therefore not cleansed by the blood of Jesus. But they will *see him* as he is and may believe in The Son of God thus justifying John 14:6.

After the thousand years are finished, the New Jerusalem comes down out of heaven from God, prepared as a bride (Christians) beautifully dressed for her husband (Revelation 21:2) to receive their reward. They are completely washed by the blood of the Lamb, free from sin.

16.

The Least in the Kingdom of Heaven

The sheep and the goats will stand before The Great Judgment.

Those who lived by the law will be judged by the law. Those who do not know the law, live by a natural law. They will be judged according to their conscience (Romans 2:12-15). The sheep will inherit the earth. The Goat will be cast into eternal damnation.

Christians will be like Christ, they will be with Him in a heavenly body.
(Philippians 3:21)

Chapter 1

Original Sin

There are numerous scenarios attempting to decipher the biblical conclusion to the ***End of Time*** according to God's Word. The problem is most theologians do not agree with each other and have trouble lining up, connecting with other prophecy that relate to end times. Many look to The Book of Revelation for answers without realizing that most of it is mirrored within the Old as well as the New Testament, while others end up with gaps in their interpretations; excluding pivotal turn of events that should have been included thereby bringing more confusion to the issue.

Original Sin

In the very beginning God created all things and He created man in His images and likeness He created them. Adam and Eve are given a world that is filled with beauty and wonder, everything they could need. Adam was placed in the garden Eden (means pleasure) to work it and care for it. What is the most appealing from all that they have received is the perfect mate to share with all that they have; they have is each other. Adam and Eve were placed in a beautiful garden with the perfect companion and were given Grace and Love from a Father who created them.

Original Sin

In the midst of the garden were the tree of life and the tree of knowledge of good and evil. God tells them "Of every tree of the garden you may freely eat; but of the tree of the knowledge of good and evil you shall not eat, for in the day that you eat of it you shall surely die." There does not seem to be a problem with these instructions until they are approached by an unwelcome presence.

Lucifer, a creation of God, considered a pinnacle in his abode, the most beautiful of all the angels, lost his position of authority in the heavenly places because he became self absorbed by his beauty and intelligence to the point that he wanted to be like God. Lucifer fell from Grace along with a myriad of followers. He is called Satan the deceiver of the world.

Original Sin

Lucifer entices Eve then Adam to the possibility that maybe God has not been completely forth coming. They are tricked by Satan's deception into accepting his offer. They eat of the tree of knowledge of good and evil. Their disobedience was one thing but there is actually more to this story. Something happen that has not been fully understood which affected Adam, Eve and their decedents, the entire world.

The Grace of God which clothed them was gone. Something else had taken its place; Adam and Eve find themselves naked. Their sin was exposing them and they cannot get rid of it.

Original Sin

Only God was able to cover their nakedness, their sin with the skins of animals. Their skins were representation of a sacrificial death for sin. This sacrifice could only cover their sin but could not eliminate it.

From this point on, the Old Testament tells us how God is very selective in everything He does and people He chooses to the point of micro managing. What He is doing is showing the world He requires perfection which is impossible for man to be perfect.

What is interesting is that God finds pleasure when individuals who realize they can never be perfect and in turn, retreating into submission, asking the Father to guide their path.

Original Sin

Men by nature are rebellious. Is man able to submit on his own or is there a need for God to assist with the ability to submit? John 6:44 answers this question.

Jesus said,

"No one can come to me unless the Father who sent me draws them"

Every word, especially those spoken directly by God, Christ, is of extreme importance and cannot be taken for granted. God Himself mentions that ***every*** Word He speaks has a purpose; it ***shall*** accomplish what He pleases and ***shall*** prosper in the thing for which it was sent.

Original Sin

In Isaiah 55:11 God said,

So shall My **word** be that goes forth from My mouth; It shall not return to Me **void**, But it shall accomplish what I please, And it shall prosper in the thing for which I sent it.

According to Christian teachings only those who believe and obey the Gospel of Jesus will be saved. But what Christians don't realize is that they are missing out on more of the meat of the Word.

Original Sin

So now we ask "Were there people from the past six thousand biblical years who deserved an opportunity to know Christ"?

Secondly, God made promises to Abraham and his decedents. How can God's covenant with O. T. Jews fit in with John 14:6?

Jesus answered, "I am the way and the truth and the life. No one comes to the Father except through me. (John 14:6)

If God is a Just and True, does He make provisions for these people of the past or did the Jews become obsolete? Romans 11:1 Paul said, "did God cast away His people; certainly not!"

Original Sin

Question: if salvation is through Christ alone, how will God's Old Testament people be saved without nullifying salvation through Christ alone?

The answers are amazingly hidden within His Word. By God's Grace these mysteries will be unraveled, brought to light for your discernment; to question, to study and to open God's Truth.

Any biblical insights about the mysteries of the Bible are from the Lord. God chooses who is to accomplish His Will. There is not one person who can claim he has insight or knowledge of any part of the bible without God's inspiration. All glory belongs to God.

I am but a simple man of no repute used as an instrument who follows the guidance of my Lord and Savior Jesus Christ to bring Glory to God.

Do not believe anything written by the Author of this book, but test every word by the fire of the Word of God.

With this said, we must question all things and hold fast to that which is true. (1st Thes. 5:21)

God's Plan

Ask any believer and most will tell you that *only* Christians are going to heaven. Christians, <u>who are</u> children of God, <u>do</u> have a place in heaven but to say no one else is considered by God is incorrect. The Jews were first to be selected by God for a reason, not to be discarded but they are included in the whole scheme of the Word of God.

Christians were last to became children of God after the crucifixion but became "first" because the Jews rejected the Christ. But according to Romans 11:5, a remnant of Jews are selected according to election. A *remnant* of millions of Jew over a 4 thousand year period could be a very significant number. Although O. T. Jews will not be saved in the same manner as Christian, (how are they able to believe in Jesus before His time) God made a provisional plan in accordance to His promise. <u>*This is what confuses Christians.*</u>

God's Plan

They, Jews were first but have become "last". God has a plan that was in place before creation.

The last will be first and the first will be last.

In the book of Acts 1, for forty days after the crucifixion, Jesus appeared and spoke to them about the Kingdom of God. The assembly of devoted followers stood before the risen Christ as He appeared to them. As He ate with them, He commanded them not to depart from Jerusalem but to wait for the gift His Father promised (The Pentecost).

God's Plan

The aposples asked, "Will You at this time restore the Kingdom to Israel?" But He said in Acts 1:7

And He said to them, "It is not for you to know times or seasons which the Father has put in His own authority.

He could have said the Kingdom will be restored to the Gentiles. But there is a drama that continues **_until_** God's plan with the gentiles is complete at which point He will commence with His plans for the Jews.

LUKE 21:24
And they (the Jews) will fall by the edge of the sword, and be led away captive into all nations. And Jerusalem will be **trampled** by Gentiles **_until_** the times of the Gentiles are fulfilled.

God's Plan

Questions to consider

*Is the Kingdom of God in spirit or flesh or both?

*If the Kingdom of God was of the flesh, what is the purpose?

*Will Jesus be The King in the Kingdom of God?

Allow the Word of God to answers these questions:

Chapter

The Deception

Satan said to Eve "DID GOD REALLY SAY, 'YOU MUST NOT EAT FROM ANY TREE IN THE GARDEN'?"

If Satan was able to trick Adam and Eve, is he able to trick faithful Christians?

The most knowledgeable students of Christ are not immune. Look at some of the more influential preachers; they are divided, unable to agree with fundamental theology; thus creates division or denominationalism.

The Deception

Before Darwin, there was no such word as _Evolution_. But it seems at times whenever Christians try to explain biblical accounts of creation in an open forum, the word evolution in thrown into the mix. Like a poison, this word eats away at any promise of convincing others that God created in 6 days. I have heard discussions among Christian believers about creation trying to rationalize how God could create in six days; that maybe there could be a possibility that it took thousands of years.

The Deception

People for the most part, consider themselves intelligent and rational. But at times we tend to reason away God's Truth a bit too much. We allow human logic to intervene, unconsciously questioning God's very Words more often than we think.

Although unintentional, they don't realize they are questioning God's Words. And like Satan, they may be saying:

"Did God really say, 'He created in six days'?"

The Deception

The controversy among some Christians over whether creation was completed in 6 days or thousands of years stems from the Book of 2ⁿᵈ Peter: "a one day is like thousand years and a thousand years is like one day." This passage has been misunderstood by many; but what's critical is that it's been misused to corrupt and mislead the very Words of God. This controversy brings confusion and doubt among believers. Peter may be saying, "whether it's a day or a thousand years it's all the same to God."

2 PETER 3:8

But do not forget this one thing, dear friends: With the Lord a day is like a thousand years, and a thousand years are like a day.

The Deception

In foresight; God's explicitly defines what He is saying.

According to Genesis 1, God distinctly mentions the words _evening_ and _morning._ The days are numbered, _first day, second day._ After reading Genesis 1, any fifth grader, would conclude that God created in 6 days.

Exodus 20:8-11 also reaffirms the days of creation as ordinary days. This is where God tells the Israelites to work for six days and rest on the seventh because God had made all things in six days and rested on the seventh.

Jesus' promise of salvation is as good today as it was 2 thousand years ago.

Chapter

God Did not Reject His People

Born again spiritually, Christian believers are cleansed by the blood; they will be presented to Christ in heaven as the Bride. (Rev.:20)

Jesus has paid the price. There is nothing else believers can do to improve this perfect salvation, except to trust and obey. The outcome is eternal peace in heaven with Jesus. But what will God do for the followers of the Old Testament according to Romans 11: (NIV)

Paul asks,

Did God reject his people? By no means, I am an Israelite myself

God Did not Reject His People

:12 their loss means riches for the Gentiles, how much greater riches will their full inclusion bring (NIV)

1st. Their loss means riches for gentiles

Christians receive the promise meant for the Jews

2nd. If Jews receive full inclusion, the

Gentile receives a much greater reward.

God Did not Reject His People

God so loved the World that He gave His
only begotten son that who so ever
believes in Him may be saved. How can
someone from the O. T. believe unless
he has heard the Gospel? Could it be
possible that in God's foresight the
scripture already addresses this issue
so that all those worthy of salvation may
have a chance to know about Jesus?

God Did not Reject His People

Believing Jesus' Words

Satan is a manipulator and loves to mislead. We have to remember he's had thousands of years to think and devise deceptive ways to bring doubt. A cunning yet wickedly brilliant way Satan confuses even the most knowledgeable of Christians, is by twisting God's Word. Satan unsuccessfully tried to persuade Jesus into submission at a most vulnerable time, offering a king's domain on earth in return. If Satan was bold enough to try to confuse the Son of God, what would make us think Satan would not use this tactic on God's children? The sad thing is Satan has better success influencing people.

God Did not Reject His People

Christians sometimes become so confident in their understanding of scripture that we stand firm on we believe. I too am guilty. Instead of submitting with a child-like mind and allowing the Word of God to lead our understanding, we box ourselves into a belief that is sometimes impenetrable. This is one reason why churches are separated into denomination.

The win/win attitude of people is natural. Wanting to get ahead is everyone's ambition which at times leaves others on the losing end. People find it hard (including myself) to let others win thereby accepting a lower position.

God Did not Reject His People

Reasons why the non-believing secular world rejects God's ways are because they view God's ways as illogical. The Bible does not make any sense to them. Jesus portrays Himself as a servant to the point of washing others feet. In fact passages like, "we must die to self in order to live in Christ" is a good example of what the secular worldly people think of Christian's beliefs as being backward, upside down, an inverted logic.

John 11:25-27

Jesus said to her, "I am the resurrection and the life. The one who believes in me will live, even though they die; and whoever lives by believing in me *will never die*. Do you believe this?"

God Did not Reject His People

Phil 2:3-11

Do nothing from rivalry or conceit, but in humility count others more significant than yourselves. Let each of you look not only to his own interests, but also to the interests of others.

To the worldly man, Christians are foolish. God's ways and thoughts are not understood by common man.

Isaiah 55:8,9

"For my thoughts are not your thoughts, neither are your ways my ways," declares the LORD.
"As the heavens are higher than the earth,
so are my ways higher than your ways and my thoughts than your thoughts.

45.

But even Christians at times have a problem approaching the Bible with a child-like mind to believe that nothing is impossible for God. As you will see in my next chapter it is very likely you may have a hard time believing what you are reading.

Chapter

Born again

Anyone unfamiliar with the Gospel would naturally wonder about this passage and possibly taking it literally, "you must be born again".

Like Nicodemus, they would ask "how can this be, how can a man enter his mother womb and be borne again".

John 3:3

Jesus replied, "Very truly I tell you, no one can see the Kingdom of God unless they are born again.

Faith is believing in something you can't see. Jesus said you cannot see it unless they are born again.

Born again

I am a spiritually *born again* Christian by believing Jesus is the Son of God, who is risen from the dead, He is seated at the right hand of the Father. This means I am spiritually in the Kingdom of God and I can only see it in my mind's eye. It is not of this world but it is in the spirit that we see the Kingdom of God. Jesus said "My Kingdom is not of this world."

John 18:36

Jesus answered, "My Kingdom is not of this world. If My kingdom were of this world, My servants would fight, so that I should not be delivered to the Jews; but now My kingdom is not from here."

John 3:5

Jesus answered, "Very truly I tell you, no one can enter the kingdom of God unless they are born of water and the Spirit.

48.

Born again

If Jesus is speaking of spiritual things there is no question and most will understand Jesus is talking about, a Spiritual Kingdom.

But if He is speaking of earthly things, not spiritual, He must be talking about something that has not happen yet because I have not physically seen the Kingdom of God. To have a physical Kingdom on earth, God would have to harness evil and take over the world.

Jesus proceeds to tell Nicodemus, "You are Israel's teacher and do you not know these things?" (John 3:10 NKJ)

Jesus said to Nicodemus, "You should know this."

49.

Born again

If the Jews should know about The Kingdom of God, Old Testament should reveal what Jesus is saying.

Jesus again gives a clued as to what He is saying:

I have spoken to you of earthly things and you do not believe; how then will you believe if I speak of heavenly things? (3:12)

Adding more mystery to what is already deep. Jesus is saying, "this Kingdom _**is**_ of an earthly matter.

If the Kingdom of God is an earthly thing, are we living in the Kingdom now? If this world is God's Kingdom why does evil flourish?

Born again

There are innumerable scriptures throughout the New Testament pointing to Old Testament promises from God to a chosen remnant. But John 14:6 tells us, *"the only way to the Father is through Christ Jesus."* There is no other way to save anyone except by the *knowledge* of Salvation through Christ.

Jesus said, "No one comes to the Father except through me." John 14:6

The natural man's answer is: this is impossible, it cannot be done. If it were possible how will God accomplish this?

<u>With man, not all things are possible but with God nothing is impossible.</u>

Let the scripture answers this question:

Chapter

Christians and Jews

In the beginning of Jesus' ministry, Jesus only concerned Himself with only the Jews. He never went outside the Judean territory. He never sought the gentiles, but they sought Jesus. Jesus never ventured outside of the people of Israel.

Matthew 15:24

He answered, "I was sent only to the lost sheep of Israel."

Christians and Jews

Matthew 10:5

[5] These twelve Jesus sent out with the following instructions: "Do not go among the Gentiles or enter any

town of the Samaritans. [6] Go rather to the lost sheep of Israel.

In the beginning Jesus was not concerned about the gentile or the rest of the world for that matter? If the Jews had accepted Jesus as the Christ and He became their King, the rest of the World would have no hope of eternal life. (Eph. 2:12)

Christians and Jews

After Jesus' resurrection, the Jews are
set aside to give way to the gentiles. It is
a mystery, why all of a sudden the gospel
seems to reject the Jews because they
believe in salvation through the Law
rather than salvation by God's grace?
But Romans 11:1 is distinct about the
promise of God.

I ask then: Did God reject his people?
By no means! I am an Israelite
myself, a descendant of Abraham,
from the tribe of Benjamin. God did
not reject his people, whom he
foreknew.

:11 salvation has come to the
Gentiles to make Israel envious.

:22 Consider therefore the kindness and sternness of God: sternness to those who fell, but kindness to you, provided that you continue in his kindness. Otherwise, you also will be cut off.

:12 But if their transgression means riches for the world, and their loss means riches for the Gentiles, *how much greater* riches *will their full* inclusion bring!

Chapter

Chosen without Knowledge

Many Corinthians who heard the Gospel believed and were baptized. It is at this point, The Lord spoke to Paul in a vision saying "do not be afraid; keep speaking, do not be silent for I am with you, no one will harm you, because <u>I have many people in the city</u>."

The Lord assures Paul that there were many in the city, but who were they, what do they know? Apparently Paul had no knowledge of them without the Lord telling him. Paul had not been there long enough to reach the inner city. He believed His mission was to convert Jews and was spending much of his time trying to convince them.

Chosen without Knowledge

Acts 18:9 (NIV)

One night the Lord spoke to Paul in a vision: "Do not be afraid; keep on speaking, do not be silent. **10** For I am with you, and no one is going to attack and harm you, because *I have many people in this city*." **11** So Paul stayed in Corinth for a year and a half, teaching them the word of God.

What is the meaning of this statement from the Lord, "I am with you ... *I have many in the city*"? Paul was aware of the many who had come to the knowledge of Christ and were baptized.

Chosen without Knowledge

But why would the Lord appear to Him and tell him something he already knows unless the Lord is telling him something he doesn't know. Obviously the Lord knows Paul's thoughts and wanted to dissuade him of his plans.

If there were many people in the city chosen by God how could they know without hearing the Gospel.

This opens an interesting observation. If there are many in the city, who are they, what about the rest of the people? Does God not care about all people? The passage "many are called but few are chosen" (Matt.22:14 NKJ) spoken by Jesus, implies a selection already chosen by God.

Chosen without Knowledge

Ephesians 1:4, 5 mentions those chosen were predestined in accordance with God's Will and Pleasure. God finds pleasure in selecting people before the creation of the world and determining what they will become, their destiny. This is an irritating idea to many Christians who find it absurd to think that God would have a direct intervention with anyone. They believe people choose God instead of the other way around. Isn't God the potter, does He not mold us the way He wants us to be?

Kingdom of God

The Bible mentions the Kingdom of God and the Kingdom of Heaven.

There is no question as to where the Kingdom of Heaven would exist, in heaven of course. The Kingdom of God could be either heaven or earth; it is wherever God has full control, it is His Kingdom.

For a physical Kingdom of God to exist on earth, God would have to take complete control of the world and Satan. This is the *first requirement*.

I present several passages pointing to a The Kingdom God, a Government established on earth by the Will and Power and of All Mighty God.

Kingdom of God

Seated on the Throne of David in Jerusalem is the King of Kings, Lord of Lords, The Christ.

Revelation 20:2

2 He laid hold of the dragon, that serpent of old, who is *the* Devil and Satan, and bound him for a thousand years; 3 and he cast him into the bottomless pit, and shut him up, and set a seal on him, so that he should deceive the nations no more till the thousand years were finished.

4 And I saw thrones, and they sat on them, and judgment was committed to them. Then *I saw* the souls of those who had been beheaded for their witness to Jesus and for the Word of God, who had not worshiped the beast or his image, and had not received *his* mark on their foreheads or on their hands. And they lived and reigned with Christ for a thousand years.

Kingdom of God

Jesus told His apostles you will rule over the twelve tribes of Israel.

Matthew 19:28
So Jesus said to them, "Assuredly I say to you, that in the *regeneration*, when the Son of Man sits on the throne of His glory, you who have followed Me will also sit on twelve thrones, judging the twelve tribes of Israel.

Zechariah 14:9, 16

The LORD will be king over the whole earth.

Then the survivors from all the nations that have attacked Jerusalem will go up year after year to worship the King, the LORD Almighty, and to celebrate the Festival of Tabernacles.

The Lord God will give him the throne of his father David, and he will reign over Jacob's descendants forever; his kingdom will never end." (Luke 1:32)

The King of Kings will rule the earth. Kingdom of God is in control of earths inhabitants. Ruled by force, if the inhabitants do not comply, they will suffer the plague. Satan is bound for a thousand years.

According to Zechariah 14, in The Kingdom of God, God establishes full control of the earth and places the King of Kings as Ruler of all the earth, while Satan is bound. People are forced to worship the King or they will be subjected to the possibility of death, dashed like pottery.

Kingdom of God

Psalm 2:4

The One enthroned in heaven laughs;
the Lord scoffs at them.

He rebukes them in his anger
and terrifies them in his wrath, saying,

"I have installed my king
on Zion, my holy mountain."

I will proclaim the LORD's decree:

He said to me, "You are my son;
today I have become your father.

Ask me,
and I will make the nations your
inheritance,
the ends of the earth your possession.

You will break them with a rod of iron;
you will dash them to pieces like
pottery."

Kingdom of God

The _second requirement_ for the Kingdom of God to exist is taken from the 1st book of Corinthians.

1st Cor.15:50.

Flesh and blood cannot inherit the Kingdom of God,

nor does the perishable inherit the imperishable.

This passage is mysterious. It is a complex divisional statement displacing two separate time periods. This passage would be considered one event if we were looking for a Heavenly Kingdom inhabited by the imperishable but the inhabitants in the Kingdom of God _will perish_ if they don't comply according to Zechariah 14.

The scripture mentions an earthly Kingdom, The Kingdom of God lasting 1000 years before The Final Judgment according to Revelation 20:1-4.

"flesh and blood cannot inherit the kingdom of God"

The second part of this statement declares *"the perishable are clothed with imperishable, with immortality"* to spend eternity with God in the Kingdom of Heaven, the place where God dwells.

If people do not have flesh and blood are they spirit?

Can God bring people back to life without blood?

Regeneration

In Ezekiel 11, God forms man from the bones of the dead people of Israel. He attaches the tendons, flesh and covers them with skin. He breathes life into them.

God said. "I will give them an undivided heart and put a new spirit in them; I will remove from them their heart of stone and give them a heart of flesh." Ezekiel 11:19, **36:26**

Ezekiel 37:12 Sovereign LORD says: My people, I am going to open your graves and bring you up from them; I will bring you back to the land of Israel.

:5 Sovereign LORD says to these bones: I will make breath[a] enter you, and you will come to life. **6** I will attach tendons to you and make flesh come upon you and cover you with skin; I will put breath in you, and you will come to life. Then you will know that I am the LORD.'"

Kingdom of God

We have just read <u>flesh and bone</u> coming together and God gives them the breath of life.

Regeneration

What did Adam say about Eve, "this is flesh of my <u>flesh and bone</u> of my bone".
(Genesis 2:23)

Jesus appeared before the apostles after the crucifixion, He had been with God. He said to Thomas, "Look at my hands and my feet. It is I myself! Touch me and see; a ghost does not have <u>flesh and bones</u>," then He asked them if they had anything to eat and He ate a piece of broiled fish in their presences. Luke 24:39-42

Adam and Eve, like Jesus were in the presence of God in *flesh and bone.*

Genesis 2:23

Chapter

Believing the Word of God

If Jesus wants us to have faith like a child, there would be no question as to what Jesus is saying. Although natural rebirth is impossible to the natural man, we accept the His Words by faith. Let's allow the Word of God to clarify.

For thousands of years men from the Old Testament era have accepted without full understand; God's Word contains mysterious passages that are undecipherable by the brightest intellect. God demands and deserves all the Glory. Only God reveals through instruments of His choosing. Yet today scholars have carelessly boxed themselves along with their followers into a corner by standing firm on their answers to passages that seem unanswerable by human logic.

Believing the Word of God

The inspired writers of the Old and New Testament did not fully understand all of what they wrote; but to confidently say today we now fully understand what we have interpreted of Word of God is saying, "***it can mean nothing else***," would be limiting ourselves to human intelligence. In limiting ourselves, we are placing barriers, closing any supernatural inspirational link with the creator.

Instead of allowing God's inspiration, to continue we are saying we have all the answers we need. To say, "To be born again can only mean spiritual baptism and nothing else" we are placing limits in God's power; closing our minds to any change or spiritual enlightenment within the mysteries of the Word of God.

Believing the Word of God

Flesh & Blood or Flesh & Bone

Flesh and blood cannot inherit the Kingdom of God. But Jesus, Adam and Eve were in the presence of God in flesh and bone. God breathed life into Adam. In Ezekiel 37:5 God breathes life into flesh and bone thus bringing a body back to life.

Flesh and blood cannot inherit the Kingdom of God (1 Cor. 15:50) but God gives life to flesh & bone and placed His newly established Kingdom (Zech 14) on earth. It becomes clear that those who will *see and enter* (John 3:3, 5) the Kingdom of God will be flesh and bone brought to life with God's breath. They have been *born again*.

Believing the Word of God

There is something about the blood that keeps us separated from God. According to the Bible, the blood has *life*, it must die, separated from the body. Flesh and bone must be free from this life from the blood.

LEVITICUS 17:11

FOR THE LIFE OF THE FLESH IS IN THE BLOOD.

Why is human life's blood so repulsive to God? There is no doubt that aspect of sin is human life's blood. This mystery seems to stem from that incident with Satan in the Garden of Eden. There is a much deeper involvement that many theological scholars refuse to delve into. It has to do with her seed and thy seed. This subject matter reaches such point that the human mind refuses to accept it. I prefer not to discuss it.

It is a scientific fact, at conception; blood is passed on to the child from only one of the parents, the father. When Jesus was conceived, His body had no blood from His mother and there was no male donor. The Life given to this Child was from God, not the life from human blood. **No Sin.** There is also mention of water mixed with the blood which came out of His side He was pierced with a spear. *Living water* is significant as in John 7:38 and Zechariah 14:8. I believe this same *living water* is used in John 3:5 when one is born again of water and the spirit. The clue that ties it all together is when Jesus said we _can_ _enter_ the Kingdom of God (John 3:5) but flesh and blood _cannot_ _enter_ the Kingdom of God (1st Corintians 15:50).

Chapter

The Kingdom of God on Earth

The LORD will be king over the whole
earth. (Zechariah 14:9)

HEBREWS 8:6

"The days are coming, declares the Lord,
when I will make a <u>new covenant</u>
<u>with the people of Israel</u>
and with the people of Judah.

10: I will put my laws in their minds
and write them on their hearts.

I will make a new covenant
with the people of Israel

Revelation 20:5   they lived and reigned
with Christ a thousand years.

The Kingdom of God on Earth

Rev. 1:5   the firstborn from the dead, and the ruler of the kings of the earth.

Luke 1:30   And He will reign over the house of Jacob forever

ISAIAH 9:7   Of the increase of his government and peace there shall be no end, upon the throne of David

The Kingdom of God on Earth

There are no Christians involved within this unfinished business on earth. God will take one thousand years to conclude the rest of His chosen people who have not known Jesus. The reason they are _born again_ to enter the Kingdom is to present them to the Christ; they will have an opportunity to see Him and believe that He is the Son of the Living God. This world event qualifies those worthy of salvation required by John 14:6

Jesus answered,

"No one comes to the Father except through me."

The New Jerusalem (Christians) will come down from heaven as the bride of Christ. This is the final entrance, the bride.

I saw the Holy City, the New Jerusalem, coming down out of heaven from God, prepared as a bride beautifully dressed for her husband.

(Revelation 21:2)

Chapter

It is Finished

Jesus makes a final declaration to the Jews before He prepares for His crucifixion.

He said of the Jews, "you will not see me again **until** you say,

'Blessed is He who comes in the name of the Lord."

It becomes clear that signs and wonder, miracles from God were not enough to change the hearts of the Jew. Before He prepares for the crucifixion, Jesus expresses the realization that He is finished with the Jews. He has finished the work He was sent to do. (John 17:4) He has done all that He could do for the Jews. They will reject Jesus and He will turn His back on them **_until_** the times of the Gentiles if fulfilled. (Luke 21:24)

It is Finished

Matthew 23:29

"They will not see Him _again_ _until_ they say: 'Blessed is He Who comes in the name of the Lord"

Longs to Gathers His Children

Matthew 23:37

"Jerusalem, Jerusalem, you who kill the prophets and stone those sent to you,

how often I have longed to gather your children together, as a hen gathers her chicks under her wings, and you were not willing.

Look, your house is left to you desolate. For I tell you, you will not see me again **_until_** you say, 'Blessed is he who comes in the name of the Lord."

It is Finished

At the end of Jesus' ministry, He has accomplished what He set out to do with the Jews. This is still a mystery to gentiles. The pervious passages emphatically predict the coming Messiah, the King of the Jews.

I do not know of one Christian minister who has preached this message. God chooses who He enables to have understanding. It is God who determines when and how His mysteries will be revealed and by whom. It is all for the Glory of God so that no man may boast.

Most Christians have a very good understanding of treasures in heaven but are unable to understand hidden mysteries. God opens the minds of those who are the least likely, the least qualified, the despised to be able see what those who claim to know but have not seen. (1st Corinthians 1:27)

:27   But God has chosen the foolish things of the world to put to shame the wise,

God has chosen the weak things of the world to put to shame the things which are mighty;

And the base things of the world and the things which are despised God has chosen,

and the things which are not, to bring to nothing the things that are,

that no flesh should glory in His presence.

It is Finished

Isaiah 45:2

I will go before you
and will level the mountains;
I will break down gates of bronze
and cut through bars of iron.

I will give you hidden treasures,
riches stored in secret places,
so that you may know that I am the
LORD,
the God of Israel, who summons you by
name.

Chapter

The Rebellion

Is God worried about the numbers, is He interested in quantity thereby compromising quality. Is the Charismatic Movement questionable? They pack into churches to hear a new easy gospel message? Preachers have become entertainers, they will sugar coat the message to please the masses. They mostly teach that God loves everybody; attracting thousands at the expense of compromising the truth by watering down the message.

The Rebellion

Whenever the Word of God is compromised, it is no longer the Word of God, it becomes a different gospel which is no gospel at all. People turn away from the truth to follow a different compromising teaching; this is what the Bible calls The Rebellion. These acts, performed by multitudes throughout the world are described as *The Rebellion (NIV)* or the *Falling Away (NKJ) from God* in 2nd Thessalonians 2:3.

"The Rebellion" (Falling Away) is a pivotal turning point of humanity. This is the Beginning of the End of Evil Times. The Man of Lawlessness (the beast) will be held back until that which is holding Him back is taken out of the way. After "The Rebellion" Christians are taken out of the way, the Holy Spirit is also taken out of the way at which point the man of lawlessness (antichrist) is presented and loved by the world thus begins the Seven Year Tribulation. (2nd Thessalonians 2)

After This

When that which is holding him back is taken out of the way, that which is evil is released to have **_his_** way with the world for seven years. (2nd Thes. 2)

What holds him back is the Holy Spirit of God. God said of His Spirit to them who belong to Him, "I will never leave or forsake you". (Hebrews 13:5) Just as the Angels would not leave Lot in Sodom and Gomorrah until He safe, in the same way Christians are taken out of the way before the man of lawlessness, the Beast presented. Once God's children are taken out of the way, there will be no more need for the Holy Spirit to remain on this evil earth; He will also be taken out of the way.

Once the Holy Spirit is removed, the world is left with non-Christians. The door is left wide open for all chaos to pour into the world who is unaware of the _subtle_ departure of Christians. There are no Christians on earth during the seven year tribulation otherwise the Holy Spirit would continue to stay for any child of God. For God said, "I will never leave or forsake you." The antichrist cannot present **_himself_** unless the Holy Spirit is taken out of the way.

Christians are taken out of the world like a thief in the night. I belief they simply die off until the last one is gone. The Holy Spirit leaves with the last Christian.

The Rebellion

According to scripture, the Jews have been blind to God's Will **_until_** something happens. The scriptures distinctly states there is fullness or a number of gentiles will come in. When this fullness or number is reached, then the next phase begins. Take special notice to the word **_until_**. Luke 21:24 mentions the Jews being trampled **_until_** the fulfillment of the gentile.

It's hard not to notice the fullness or full of number gentiles implies a limit. It also implies that there is a magical number more than likely an exact number. When you fill a glass with water to its fullness it will run over. You cannot add another drop otherwise it overflows.

The Rebellion

Romans 11:25

that blindness in part is happened to
Israel, ***until*** the fulness of the Gentiles
be come in KJV

Israel has experienced a hardening in
part *until* the full number of the Gentiles
has come in NIV

Luke 21:24

And they will fall by the edge of the
sword, and be led away captive into all
nations. And Jerusalem will be trampled
by Gentiles ***until*** the times of the
Gentiles are fulfilled. NKJ

Chapter

Free Will

If Jesus said "_No one_ comes to the Father except through Me,"(John 14:6);

Are there any exceptions?

As far as **_"Free Will"_** is concerned, if Jesus said

"_No one_ can come to Me

unless the Father who sent Me draws him" John 6:44

Are there exceptions to this statement; can a person draw himself to God?

Scriptures are irrefutable. The Word of God is to be without end.

90.

Free Will

The more we study the more God's Word the more it inspires.

But if these passages I have quoted have not convinced you?

Jesus said it one more time to reaffirm that it is not our will that leads us to salvation but God's Will.

"no one can come to me unless the Father has enabled them."

John 6:65

Chapter

The Lord Returns

Here is one (of many) mystery from the Bible which kept the fire of the Word of God unquenched, leading to the writing this book.

Zechariah 14

A day of the LORD is coming, Jerusalem, when your possessions will be plundered and divided up within your very walls.

I will gather all the nations to Jerusalem to fight against it; the city will be captured, the houses ransacked, and the women raped. Half of the city will go into exile, but the rest of the people will not be taken from the city.

The Lord Returns

Then the LORD will go out and fight against those nations, as he fights on a day of battle. On that day His feet will stand on the Mount of Olives, east of Jerusalem, and the Mount of Olives will be split in two from east to west, forming a great valley, with half of the mountain moving north and half moving south. You will flee by my mountain valley, for it will extend to Azel.

On that day there will be neither sunlight nor cold, frosty darkness. It will be a unique day—a day known only to the LORD—with no distinction between day and night. When evening comes, there will be light.

93.

The Lord Returns

On that day ***living water*** will flow out from Jerusalem, half of it east to the Dead Sea and half of it west to the Mediterranean Sea, in summer and in winter.

The LORD will be king over the whole earth. On that day there will be one LORD, and his name the only name.

This is the plague with which the LORD will strike all the nations that fought against Jerusalem: Their flesh will rot while they are still standing on their feet, their eyes will rot in their sockets, and their tongues will rot in their mouths. On that day people will be stricken by the LORD with great panic.

The Lord Returns

Then the survivors from all the nations that have attacked Jerusalem will go up year after year to worship the King, the LORD Almighty, and to celebrate the Festival of Tabernacles.

The Lord Returns

Christians washed by the blood of the Jesus are free from all sin. If a person is free from all sin, who will accuse him, what sin? There can be no judgment against one who is free from all sin. But those reborn during the Millennium both Jew and gentile still carry their sins; they are those whom Jesus calls My sheep. They are judged by the Law or they are judged according to their conscience. (Romans 2:12-15)

After the thousand years are finished, the New Jerusalem comes down out of heaven from God, prepared as a *bride* (Christians) beautifully dressed for her husband (Revelation 21:2) to receive their reward, while the sheep and the goats stand before The Great Judgment.

The Lord Returns

Those who lived by the law will be judged by the law. Those who have no law will be judged according to their conscience (Romans 2:15). The sheep will inherit the earth. The Goat will be cast into eternal damnation.

Christians will be like Christ, they will be like Him, with Him in a heavenly body. (Philippians 3:21)

The Kingdom of God

Zechariah 14:12 speaks that all nations will be against Israel in battle. At the point when total annihilation seems imminent, a flesh rotting plague destroys all who have fought against it. There will be survivors.

On that day The Lord stands on the Mount of Olives, and the world falls into the hands of The Almighty. Satan is bound for a thousand years and the King of Kings inherits the Throne of David. *This is the Kingdom of God*.

The Lord Returns

Jesus said, "_No one can see_ the Kingdom unless he is born again."

Nicodemus asked. "Surely they cannot enter a second time into their mother's womb to be born again."

Again Jesus said, "_No can enter_ the Kingdom of God unless He is born of water and spirit" (this is the living water) Jesus said, "God will give you living water. The water that I shall give him will become in him a fountain of water springing up into everlasting life." (John 4:10)

Again Jesus said to Nicodemus, "_I speak to of earthly things_, (you are a teacher) _you should know this_"

The Law

Christians search the scripture to please God. They place their faith and hope in very words that teach faith alone in Christ will save them.

Although we do not live by the Law of Moses, we live by grace through faith and follow the written Word of God with rules to follow which is a law in itself, The Law of Grace. Both Christian and Jew follow God's instructions.

The subservient law, the Law of Moses came first but became secondary to the Law of Grace. Those who live by this Law will be Judged according to the law. But those who reject God's Word are condemned

The Law

There is a third group who have no instruction they have never heard God's Word. Yet every person with a good mind knows what is good. It is indwelled in us because we are made in the image

of God. They who do not have the law (of God) but *by nature* do what is require by the law which is written in their hearts, they are a law to themselves. By nature they know it is wrong to steal, they know it is wrong to kill. This is the natural law. Those who live by the natural law will be judged according to their consciences. (Romans 2:12-16)

Judgment falls upon those who are under the Law and those who live by the natural law. Like Adam and Eve, they cannot get rid of their sin on their own without believing in the perfect sacrifice of Jesus.

The Law

What are we to say then? Are all condemned who have not heard of Jesus?

According to Romans 2, the natural man who is worthy, will be judged according to his conscience. But in God's foresight, in order to comply with John 14:6, God will breathe life into flesh and bone in order that they may live in the Kingdom of God. (Ezekiel 37) They will be subjected to The King and given an opportunity to worship The Son of God according to Zechariah 14.

In order to be in the presence of God one must be free from all sin.

The requirement to escape eternal condemnation is to believe Christ the Son of God.

The Law

By faith Christian are washed, completely cleans of all sins. They will be able to stand in the presence of God.

They who are born again in the Kingdom of God do not know of the death burial and resurrection. They are the sheep who stand in Judgment they carry their sins.

All sinners will stand in Judgment before God. All have sinned and fall short of the Glory of God. But anyone who is completely cleansed of sin will not be judged. Who can accuse them if they have no sin?

The Law

Judgments are for those who are not cleansed by the blood of Christ. The Jews who have the Law only cover their sin with animal blood sacrifice, they carry their sins, just as those who will be Judged by their conscience.

Romans 2:6 God said, "I will repay each person according to what they have done." To those who by persistence in doing good seek glory, honor and immortality, he will give eternal life. But for those who are self-seeking and who reject the truth and follow evil, there will be wrath and anger. There will be trouble and distress for every human being who does evil: first for the Jew, then for the Gentile; _but glory, honor and peace for **everyone** who does good_: first for the Jew, then for the Gentile. For God does not show favoritism. _Romans 2:6_

Chapter

The First Day of a New Beginning

This description depicts a day is coming when God has had enough with evil in the world. *The fullness of the gentiles is complete*. This means that God plan for the gentiles have been accomplished; it is finished.

So then begins the next phase in preparation for the Jews which account for the final 7 years predicted in the Book Daniel. Jesus spoke of the fulfillment of this prophecy from Daniel in Matthew 24:

Jesus said of this time period, "For then there will be great distress, unequaled from the beginning of the world until now—and never to be equaled again."

³ As Jesus was sitting on the Mount of Olives, the disciples came to him privately. "Tell us," they said, "when will this happen, and what will be the sign of your coming and of the end of the age?"

⁴ Jesus answered: "Watch out that no one deceives you. ⁵ For many will come in my name, claiming, 'I am the Messiah,' and will deceive many. ⁶ You will hear of wars and rumors of wars, but see to it that you are not alarmed. Such things must happen, but the end is still to come. ⁷ Nation will rise against nation, and kingdom against kingdom. There will be famines and earthquakes in various places. ⁸ All these are the beginning of birth pains.

9 "Then you will be handed over to be persecuted and put to death, and you will be hated by all nations because of me. 10 At that time many will turn away from the faith and will betray and hate each other, 11 and many false prophets will appear and deceive many people. 12 Because of the increase of wickedness, the love of most will grow cold, 13 but the one who stands firm to the end will be saved. 14 And this gospel of the kingdom will be preached in the whole world as a testimony to all nations, and then the end will come.

15 "So when you see standing in the holy place 'the abomination that causes desolation,'[a] spoken of through the prophet Daniel—let the reader understand— 16 then let those who are in Judea flee to the mountains. 17 Let no one on the housetop go down to take anything out of the house. 18 Let no one in the

field go back to get their cloak. [19] How dreadful it will be in those days for pregnant women and nursing mothers! [20] Pray that your flight will not take place in winter or on the Sabbath. [21] For then there will be great distress, unequaled from the beginning of the world until now— and never to be equaled again.

**

These terrible times are the worst thing that has ever happened to the Jews. There has never been or ever will be anything like it. This event happens during the Seven Year Tribulation. *The return of Christ or The Day of the Lord* is described in Zechariah 14. It begins on the last day of The Seven Year Tribulation when all Evil is harness for a time. But first a commentary:

The First Day of a New Beginning

Whole sections from the Bible have been pushed aside or neglected because it's not understood or it doesn't fit the pattern of what many have interpreted to be end times interpretations.

The time will come when God has taken control of this world which becomes the Kingdom of God. This is the Kingdom Jesus spoke of in John 3

Jesus replied, "Very truly I tell you, no one can **_see_** the kingdom of God unless they are born again.

Jesus answered, "Very truly I tell you, no one can **_enter_** the kingdom of God unless they are born of water and the Spirit.

I have spoken to you of **_earthly things_** and you do not believe; how then will you believe if I speak of heavenly things?

When this time comes, evil is harness by force, by God.

Evil will rule the Earth no more.

The First Day of a New Beginning

A world living in chaos will come to an abrupt end. No longer will people be able to do as they please. People in this new life will submit to the Highest Authority, a King in the Kingdom of God. For those who submit they will have nothing to fear. But those who reject and rebel will be they are force to comply, submitting to a supernatural power or face death.

This *New Life* is the beginning of healing for who are worthy but who were not saved because they never knew Jesus as Savior. They are given an opportunity to see the Kingdom of God. They are born again in order to enter the Kingdom of God. They are able to witness with their own eyes, The Lord of Lords The King of Kings. The purpose is to see and believed that this King is the Son of God. Through this they will be preserved for everlasting life.

They will inherit the earth

The First Day of a New Beginning

Every Word of God is important. Let the Bible open up our closed minds like a child listening to a loving protective parent.

***

The First Day of a New Beginning

According to Zechariah 14

A day of the LORD is coming,
Jerusalem, when your possessions
will be plundered and divided up
within your very walls.
I will gather all the nations to
Jerusalem to fight against it; the city
will be captured, the houses
ransacked, and the women raped.
Half of the city will go into exile, but
the rest of the people will not be
taken from the city.
Then the LORD will go out and fight
against those nations, as he fights on
a day of battle.

113.

On that day his feet will stand on the Mount of Olives, east of Jerusalem, and the Mount of Olives will be split in two from east to west, forming a great valley, with half of the mountain moving north and half moving south.

On that day there will be neither sunlight nor cold, frosty darkness. It will be a ***unique day***—a day known only to the LORD—with no distinction between day and night. When evening comes, there will be light.

On that day *living water* will flow out from Jerusalem, half of it east to the Dead Sea and half of it west to the Mediterranean Sea, in summer and in winter.

The LORD will be king over the whole earth.

Jerusalem will be inhabited; *never again* will it be destroyed.

This is the plague with which the LORD will strike *all* the nations that fought against Jerusalem: Their flesh will rot while they are still standing on their feet, their eyes will rot in their sockets, and their tongues will rot in their mouths.

115.

Then the *survivors* from all the nations that have attacked Jerusalem will go up year after year to worship the King, the LORD Almighty, and to celebrate the Festival of Tabernacles.

The LORD will bring on them the plague he inflicts on the nations that do not go up to celebrate the Festival of Tabernacles.

On that day there will *no longer be a Canaanite in the house of the LORD Almighty.*

***

116.

Notes

www.ingramcontent.com/pod-product-compliance
Lightning Source LLC
Chambersburg PA
CBHW061739020426
42331CB00006B/1292